The Patel Sisters

Shobana Patel

Ursula Patel

Copyright © 2017 THE PATEL SISTERS

All rights reserved

ISBN-13: 978-1-9998104-0-5

soul: the incorporeal essence of a living being.

mate: the partner of a living being.

DEDICATION

We dedicate this book to those who *have loved*

To those who are *in-love*

To those who *will love* in the future

To those who know that *love is real*

To all those *soulmates* out there in this world

Your journey is understood by us

ACKNOWLEDGMENTS

Two souls left an indelible mark on ours

Both are wholly responsible for what follows

CONTENTS

This book has no contents page

There are no chapters

No collections

There is no need for order

Chaos is charming

Just 100 pieces of writing

Different lengths

Different styles

Different messages

All about *soulmates*

The most chaotic connection of all

THE BEGINNING

DANGEROUS DOWN THERE

You brought me to my knees

Just be careful when I stand back up

I had a lot of time to think down there

PAST LIVES

I knew I was in trouble that day

You know *that day*

That day I realized

You were not just the love of my life

You are the love of *all of my lives*

100 NIGHTS

One night next to you

Is like 100 nights next to another

It is not that he is any less than you

It is that god designed you with me in mind

BLOOD

Everyone says *blood is thicker than water*

Indeed, that is true

We are by no means related

But if you cut me

I bleed *you*

IT BACKFIRED

Your silence takes a piece of my soul each day

Soon there will be no pieces left

Then what will you do ?

How will you entertain yourself ?

PRISONER

I am a prisoner to my addiction

My addiction is you

Now I suffer from this affliction

What am I to do ?

TUG OF WAR

One took my body

The other took my soul

I am now confused

Neither had my heart

I hated them both

DRUNK HEART

They say *a sober heart never speaks the truth*

I think they may be right

For now that I am drunk on you

I am as free as a kite

Nothing can wean me off this drug

But that is fine by me

For now that I am drunk on love

I speak the truth often and so freely

REMEMBER ?

Do you remember *that day* ?

That day you stole my heart

What a short memory you have

You shamelessly tore it apart

That which I had protected for years

No other could do that which you did

So shamelessly you took that which was not yours

But you say you don't recall

If you have no intention of loving it

Please give it back and spare a thought

For that day you stole my heart and tore it apart

DNA

Cut me

You won't find blood

For I now bleed you

You are in my DNA

The double-stranded helix is a symbol

Of how we wind around each other

Twisted and anti-parallel

ON-OFF

The reason we keep repeating

Our *on-off* cycle

Is because

Our soul

Is trying to tell us

That we are not quite done

RESCUE

I am drowning

Drowning under the magnificence of *us*

Please come and rescue me

RUINED

You ruined me for all others

That was always your intention

But as the saying goes

One man's trash

Is another man's treasure

I am now showered with his attention

IRRATIONAL

Let us not try to rationalize this

You want to speak about it and *talk it through*

But this only serves to confuse our souls

For our souls vibrate their own language

No amount of analyzing or speaking

Will allow us to understand the complexity of *us*

SILENCE

They say *actions speak louder than words*

But it's what you don't say

That really punctures me inside

Who ever knew

That silence can be such a dangerous ride

ROVING EYE

You should be here to protect me

From the *roving eye* of others

But instead

You just sit back

And despise

IT'S A PROCESS

Falling in love is a *process*

It is not an end result

It is an accumulation

Of thousands of small

Uneventful interactions

Interactions that are

Both positive and negative

When added together

These interactions

Lead to the big event

I LOVE YOU

So brace yourself

For the course of true love

Never did run smooth

SCARRED

Blinded by the tears that fell for you

Burnt by the memory of your lips

No where to hide the tears

No way to heal the burns

Forever scarred

EYES

Eyes are for seeing

They are the best part of your being

They are not a weapon to stare

So why do you pierce me with your glare

WEALTH

I do not have much

My purse is empty

My pockets are light

Not the kind of girl you can take home at night

I represent the direct opposite of you

But

The thing is

My heart is rich

Because it is full of memories

That makes me indefinitely wealthier than you

PSYCHIC SOUL

Only our soul knows if we have a tragic ending

You try to work it out with your mind

I try to solve it with my heart

But in the end

Our soul has the last laugh

WITHOUT

Without the sun there is no light

Without the moon there is no night

Without the sand there is no sea

Without you, there is *no me*

ELECTRICITY

You had galaxies in your eyes

And electricity crackled within you

The type of electricity that can light up a city

And simultaneously electrocute me

Electrocute me in ways that will make me fearful

So that I would fear all light ever again

At times, you even scared yourself

PLEASURE

My body is not merely for your pleasure

I am not here

Merely to satisfy your base needs

I will only give it you

When you touch my soul

For that is when I get the greatest pleasure

RIPPLE EFFECT

When I hear your name

I become the child

Who is standing on the river bank

Ready to throw a pebble

There is excitement

There is fear

As the pebble hits the water

The ripples flow in concentric perfection

That is what it's like hearing your name

The sound reverberates through my body

And rouses my sleeping soul

INVISIBLE TRAP

You hate me

You do not live near me

You do not see me

We are many miles apart

But you are trapped

Because each and every night

When you go to sleep

I am there to remind you in your dreams

Of what could be

ENERGY

They all say *you are handsome*

You give most ladies goosebumps

With those dashing good looks

And body to die for

Most ladies will gush

But not me

I see the light in your eyes

They shine like a beacon of hope

I want you

Not because of your dashing good looks

Nor body to die for

But because of the energy within

CLICK

You promised me the world

Big talk

But anyone can talk big

Behind a screen

Click

Click

Click

Anyone can talk big

When they let their fingers do the typing

Come out from behind that screen

And let's see if you can *walk the talk*

Or can you just click, click, click

THE WANDERER

When my mind wanders

It always comes back to the thought of you

The thought of you keeps me up all night

As I try to fall asleep in the wonder of you

SIGHT

These eyes were meant to *see you*

Day and night my thoughts return

Return to the first day our eyes met

It was that day when the dust settled

That I was able to finally see that which

Had been hidden in the dust of history

I saw that which I was meant to see

VALENTINE

Make sure you are with someone special

Someone who makes you forget which day it is

Someone who convinces you

That every day is the 14th of February

THE BOND

Our bond transcends that of *husband and wife*

That union is conditional upon marriage

Ours on the other hand is not

We can not be divorced

TICKET

My love for you is a *one-way* ticket

Will it lead me to heaven or hell ?

GIRL POWER

Society has led you to believe

That you are more powerful than me

For a man can take a woman's body with ease

But what you don't seem to realize darling

Is that I can break you in half

Without even touching you

Because when it comes to it

A woman can bypass the body for the heart

And that is when you lose

BAD REPAIR

Piece by piece he fixed me

Whilst at the same time tearing me apart

Such was the power of his love

STORY

Eyes can tell a story words can not

Human language is not developed enough

To convey what we feel when our eyes lock

So honey, stop talking and keep looking

SURVIVAL

You came

You saw

You conquered

You crushed my heart

You consumed my body

You muddled my mind

But

I survived you

That is my ultimate achievement

DENIAL

Deny me

Deny a great gift

Deny me and you deny us

Deny us and you deny freedom

Freedom from the conditioning of family

Freedom from the harness of society

Freedom from the shackles of life

HELLO

You had me at *hello*

Many people say that about many people

But, you had me at hello

You had me *in-between*

And, you will have me until the end

Of this wondrous journey of life

For it is you and you alone

Who will have me at *good-bye*

LEECH

Little did I know

That you feed off my energy

Day by day

Like a greedy leech

Sucking away

I now agree

It is best you stay away

WIN OR LOSE ?

Let's get this straight

You think you are winning

By having the last word

What you don't realize is

I have something to remember you by

Your last word keeps me company

You on the other hand

Have nothing to go by

When trying to remember me

PATIENCE

What took you so long ?

I have been waiting

All of *our lives*

TIMELESS

Falling in love with you is a *classic*

We will never go *out of style*

We are a *timeless* work of art

We are the *investment* of a lifetime

We could be sold at an auction

BIRD LOVE

Everyone says *love is eternal*

But, I say *eternal is not the right word*

For all the love I encounter

Simply flies away like a bird

TICK-TOCK

Seconds blend into minutes

Minutes blend into hours

Hours blend into days

Days spin into weeks

I hope I do not lose a year of my life

Lost in the thoughts of you

CUFFLINKS

We are like a pair of cufflinks

They make any shirt glorious

Unless of course you lose one of them

In which case they serve no purpose

DREAMS

In my dreams you stroked my hair

You said *don't worry honey it will be fine*

Reality woke me and you were not there

Please visit me again tonight

To show me you still care

DANGEROUS

You are like a sparkler honey

Exciting yet slightly dangerous

You should come with a hazard warning

SCIENCE CLASS

I can't prove it with science

But this connection we have is real

As real as anything in the periodic table

LAST MAN STANDING

I may not be your first kiss

But I certainly will be your last

For in the end

Regardless of battles

Only one wins the war

I will be the *last man standing*

And you my darling will be in awe

GOOD-BYE ?

You keep saying *good-bye*

But what you don't seem to realize is

It's never goodbye between us

It is always I will *see you later*

SLEEPLESS

I am so tired of you

It keeps me up at night

FRIEND-ZONE

The moment our eyes met

I knew then what we were

We flew straight out of the *friend-zone*

Stop trying to put us back into that box

Some things *are what they are*

SOUL-DANCE

When I saw you for the first time

I understood in that very moment

That life as I knew it would never be the same

How could it be ?

My heart stopped

And my soul danced

All in the very same moment

KOHL

Just as the kohl under my eyes is a barrier

A barrier to my tears

It can also draw a line across us

A line that you should not cross

LOSER

I have never lost at anything in my life

Until the last time I met you

For try as I might

Fight as I may

There was no way

I would be able to keep you in sight

You could not be mine

I knew that when you said *goodbye*

From the tone of your voice

That I had lost

TREMBLE

As I run my hand through your hair

I wonder if the tremble I feel

Is your soul or mine ?

I can't tell

It all feels the same to me

NATURE

My mind floats like a butterfly

At the very thought of you

My mouth buzzes like a bee

At the sound of your voice

When you are close by

My heart sings like a nightingale

When you touch me

My soul canters like a race-horse

BRICKS

Like a ton of bricks

It will hit you

It will fast become apparent

While you climb out of the rubble

The rubble that you caused

That you lost her

All you can do now

Is dust yourself off

And wish her well from afar

OPPORTUNITY

You had the opportunity

To take my soul

But that was lost

So he came along

And took that which was yours

He took my body

My mind and heart

But I feel there is still an opportunity

For he couldn't fully touch my soul

KILLING

You are killing me softly

What a sweet death

FIX-ME

With you I am whole

Without you I am broken

Please come and fix these broken pieces

And make me whole again

BEDTIME

You make me want to stay in bed for loving you

But then again

You make me want to stay in bed

For hating you

So I may as well just stay in bed

BLUE-EYES

It is so easy to get lost in a sea full of people

But your bright blue-eyes are a lighthouse

Signaling my path

You always seem to guide me home

BATH-TIME

As I wash away the days sins

The water smashes against my naked body

And then it hits me like a crashing wave

I am only a *woman* to you

And tomorrow my battle continues

To prove to you

That I deserve to be *your woman*

NOT-TINDER

I don't want to have an *encounter* with you

I want to *drown* you with my *audacity*

I want to *suffocate* your *ego*

I want to *embellish* you with my *passion*

I want to *engulf* you with my *soul*

SPARK

We are like a *tinderbox* honey

One spark and we can set the world alight

Such is the intensity of our passion

HORIZON

The sky is blue and you are you

The grass is green and I am me

It matters not that we are different

What matters is that we co-create

A breathtaking horizon when we meet

ONE SOUL

They say *eyes are the window to the soul*

I agree

When you look into mine

Pause

And look deeply

For you will clearly see

Your past, present and future

All rolled into one

Then

And only then

Will you come to accept the truth

Your soul and mine

Are one

AU NATUREL

As nature intended

A bare woman

Sans make up

If often the barer of ultimate truth

That's why you like me without make-up

Bare and raw

Adorned with only lust for you

You can't buy that in a department store

RAIN

As the rain smashes against the window pane

It reminds me of that day

That day I fell *in-love* with you

My lucid memory never lets me forget

The first moment I met you

I knew we would be forever connected

Like the rain amongst the clouds

And like the clouds

I will disappear from time to time

But we will always be connected

NO SMILE

The pain you cause this soul

Each time you run away

Can only be seen through my eyes

For you are blind

Blind to that which pains you

Sadness is now my norm

I no longer understand its opposite

Oh how I wonder

Wonder how it would feel to smile again

MOVE ON

It is easy for you to say *just move-on*

You will find somebody, you say

You then went out and did just that

But that's ok by me

If you want to shroud yourself in cotton wool

Go ahead

After all, that ego of yours bruises easily

I however, do not need to *move-on* unnecessarily

I was born a risk-taker and will remain so

Till the day I die

You see

Unlike you

I wear my bruises with pride

For they are my dignity

CONVENIENCE

Never ever

Ever, ever

Marry only for the convenience of your lifestyle

It will of course be very comfortable

But your soul will haunt you forever

It is not fair on you

Nor me

Nor her

For it is not your destiny

SHATTERED

You shattered me

The moment those words left your lips

We are better off as just good friends

So I have only to ask you this

Was everything you told me a complete lie?

How about the kiss?

Did you not feel anything?

Because

From where I was standing

Nothing could be truer

Than the promise your lips left on mine

CONNECTION

I do not seek a *boyfriend* or *lover*

I seek *a connection* beyond the norm

The type that makes my heart skip a beat

And puts a smile on my face

As soon as he walks into the room

The sort of connection that resonates

With the vibration of my soul

The type of connection that is unexplainable

This is why he is so precious to me

Because he is my *ultimate connection*

DESTINY

If it is in my destiny

The lost-love will return

So I may as well enjoy the ride

For what is meant to be will be

In this journey to my ultimate destiny

PAINT-BOX

Paint me with the entirety of you

For your love is bright

Paint a rainbow over me

For your passion is multi-colored

Let me experience the entirety of you

But beware of the explosion within my soul

For I will just as easily

Paint you with the entirety of me

For I too am a multi-colored entity

TRAIN STATION

He and I

Two broken souls

In the middle of an empty platform

We were on the floor

On our knees

Tears rolling down our eyes

How did we get to this stage of *good-bye* ?

Till we meet again

Perhaps not soon in time

But I have saved a space for you

On another platform

In another lifetime

ARMOUR

When I stand back up

From this lowly position

That you so shamelessly placed me in again

You better believe me

When I say

This is the last time I will go down there

For this time

When I stand back up

From this lowly position

I have the amour of experience

Protecting me from you

ONE DAY

One day

You will become

A distant memory

You see

I am not the type of woman

Who dwells on her past

Rather I am

The type of woman

Who walks forward

Bravely into her future

PART-TIME

You do not

I repeat, *do not*

Have the privilege

Of coming and going as you please

I do not

I repeat, *do not*

Need a part-time lover

It is all

Or nothing at all

Take it

Or

Leave it

UNWORTHY

I have always felt unworthy

Unworthy of your love

For you put yourself up high

Way up high on a pedestal

Out of reach

Too high for me I thought

Not even a ladder will get to you

But, the truth is

I am worthy of you

Unlike those other women

I am not afraid to climb that ladder

Because when one is unworthy

The only way is up

REASON

There *must* be a reason

A *real* reason

Why our tears turned into rivers

Why our hearts were pulled apart

Why our minds were dismantled

We took such delight in the abuse

The abuse we inflicted on ourselves

There surely must be a reason

STOP

When you were here

I tried to stop

A million times I tried

It seemed my heart vibrated

Only to the sound of your voice

A million times I tried

But it didn't stop

Now you are gone

It still won't stop

THE CROSSING

Let there be no crossing in this world

That separates us

May you always hold my hand

Regardless of how far we have to reach

One day the daily dream

Will become our reality

In the meantime my darling

May you find a way to reach over the crossing

And, do not let go of my hand

DIARY

When a man tells you

That you are the only woman

The *only woman* he opens up to

And when he actually opens up

Really opens up

You are very special indeed

You are his diary

A place his soul can bleed

RAPE

Even though

You did not lay a finger on me

You somehow managed

To rape my soul

KNOWING

How much do I love you ?

This much *I do not know*

How much pain have you caused me ?

This much *I do not know*

When will the wait end ?

This much I *do not know*

You are my ultimate destiny

This much I *<u>do</u> know*

PETRIFIED

When you look into my eyes

You will see everything you desire

And

This ability to see

Is exactly what petrifies you

Because when you look into my eyes

You glance deep into my soul

And

In an instant

You understand your heart and mine

This ability to see

Would scare even me

WIFE

Do not come back to me

To satisfy your basic needs

That is child's play honey

Come back

When you are ready

Ready to make me

That which you deep down

Have always wanted me to be

Come back

When you are ready

Ready to make me

Your wife

RIGHT OR WRONG ?

You are not acceptable to me

Nor to my friends or family

We both know what we have is wrong

But what can I do ?

If the heart accepts

That which is so wrong

I have no power over this force

It doesn't care about my views

Nor those of my friends or family

Day by day

Hour by hour

The heart has the power

To make that which is so wrong

My only right

ART-WORK

Wherever you are

I am always there

Without you

I will despair

Like a wave and a shore

We will meet with a crash

Our sore hearts will surely clash

But we will never part

I promise this to you

For we are *art*

PILLOW TALK

Each and every night

We talk for hours on end

We look into each others eyes

You brush the hair from my face

I stroke your cheeks

And we talk

Talk about everything

Our deepest and darkest secrets

It feels wonderful

To talk without judgment

To be open and fearless

Then we wake up

You next to her and me next to him

And we realize

It was just another dream

SEARCH PARTY

I went out looking for you

From a very young age

I was told by friends and family

The man for you is out there

So I went out looking

Keeping my eyes open at all times

High and low

I kept searching

But then I realized

Had I stopped and looked deep into my eyes

I would have found you

You were there all along

Because whatever my soul is made of

yours and mine are the same

BLEED-INK

Until I met you there was no book

The tables have now turned

Once you wanted to pin me down

Now I have pinned you to paper

All is fair in love and war

Forever etched in my memory

I now bleed ink

THERAPY

Writing is my therapy

It is the greatest gift I can give to myself

To put my thoughts to pen and paper

And

Because I never actually stopped loving you

Not only can I write

I dare say I can write an entire book

(or two) about you

So you see my love

Your departure which once left a hole

Well now it leaves me *whole*

You always saw my potential

Now I see it too

JULY 2016: LONDON

Somehow we ended up in the most iconic city in the world. It was always my childhood dream to live in London but today was just a day trip. A day trip in which time stood still.

Sat next to each-other, his sky-blue eyes met mine which are chocolate brown. At no point did the sky and chocolate part.

His glare pierced through my soul and then before I knew it his lips touched mine. I could hear our hearts beat so fast I thought I would explode. Was I dreaming ?

He then whispered:
I know you have been waiting for that for a long time.
I wanted to say: *yes I have, two years to be precise you horrible, gorgeous man.*
Instead I said*: I have been nervous all day.*
He replied: *yes I know.*

I grabbed his hand and in that moment knew we were meant to be. All else was a game…

Excerpt from Ursula's next book
Diary of a Soulmate
www.instagram.com/emotioncanvas

THE PROMISE

I know you are scared
But there is no way out of this *janeman*
The promise was made long ago
Long before the others arrived
If you remain still for just one moment
The faint memory will return
Remember now ?
Our souls made a promise long before we met

In this lifetime
We are merely preparing ourselves
Preparing for our final reunion
Others may look upon us as *new lovers*
But they do not know about *the promise*

As soon as you send me a signal I will come
I have to come
We have no choice in the matter
We must fulfill our promise

[*janeman* is the hindi word for *sweetheart*]

Excerpt from Shobana's next book
Pyaar, Ishq aur Mohabbat:
A Collection Inspired by Bollywood
www.instagram.com/the.indian.poet

COINCIDENCE

There are over 7 billion people

On this wondrous planet of ours

And I get to meet you

Even if there were 7 billion more

I would still get to meet you

For ours is a story of destiny

One that statistics can not explain

In another place

Another lifetime

Things would still be the same

We put coincidence to shame

THE END

This book had no contents page

There were no chapters

No collections

We felt there was no need for order

Because, we believe *chaos is charming*

There were just 100 pieces of writing

Different in length

Different in style

Each with a different message

All however

About *soulmates*

The most chaotic connection of all

This page is for our readers. An invitation to write your thoughts, express your feelings and share the story of your soul. Take a photo of this page once completed and email it to us. We will feature all photos on our social media pages. We would also love to see a photo of you with our book.
Thank you for all your support !

[wearethepatelsisters@gmail.com]

SHOBANA

Shobana is a creative wordsmith, urban philosopher and historical storyteller. Through her multidisciplinary work she observes the contradictions and fractures that have arisen in our 21st century society, commentates on the behavioral aspects of our individual and collective psychology and harnesses the teachings of forgotten philosophes and spirituality to motivate, inspire and provoke change.

URSULA

Ursula is an all round creative writer and contemporary artist. Through her social media presence she captures the audiences attention through quotes and poems on the elusive topics of love, relationships and emotions. She directs some of her time online to discussing issues related to disability, body image and self-confidence in an aim to inspire others.

We *see* therefore we write
We *feel* therefore we write
We *think* therefore we write
We *write* therefore we are
We *are* <u>The Patel Sisters</u>

SOULMATE

soulmate: a person with whom you have an immediate connection; the 'yin' to your 'yang'.

Printed in Great Britain
by Amazon